ROBESON STREET

Other books of poetry by Fanny Howe include:

EGGS
THE AMERINDIAN COASTLINE POEM
POEM FROM A SINGLE PALLET
ALSACE LORRAINE
FOR ERATO: THE MEANING OF LIFE

ROBESON STREET

poems by
Fanny Howe

Alice James Books

Copyright © 1985 by Fanny Howe

Book cover and design by Colleen McCallion
Typesetting by Xanadu Graphics
Photograph by Ben Watkins

The publication of this book was made possible with
support from the National Endowment for the Arts,
Washington, D.C., and from the Massachusetts Council
on the Arts and Humanities, a state agency whose funds
are recommended by the Governor and appropriated by
the State Legislature.

Grateful acknowledgment is made to the editors of the
following periodicals, in which some of these poems first
appeared: *Boxcar, Temblor, Ironwood* and *How(ever)*.

This book is from and for: Ilona Karmel, Hans Zucker
and Father Robert Moran.

Library of Congress Catalogue Card Number
ISBN 0-914086-58-8 (hardbound)
ISBN 0-914086-59-6 (paperback)

Alice James Books are published by the Alice James
Poetry Cooperative, Inc.

Alice James Books
138 Mt. Auburn Street
Cambridge, Massachusetts 02138

CONTENTS

ROBESON STREET

The moon is moving away
As civilization advances without thought
For the consequences

Scattered snow showers put fine purfling
Around the edges of the lot

If I handle routines, I'll dream longer
Since the concord I long for
Is like not being alive but finished

Moonlight at a fountain
For extra cash and you won't see one ideology
Funnel the soda

But continued actions will improve your looks
You whose last customer was Disappointment

After I'm done with it, the counter's
got a lovely brown finish

Solitary, I set up a night fork
And face the materials

On Robeson Street, the red oak trees
have dropped their leaves

around the rough
but indoor tables.

And I'll never plan again
to clean a house where nature's in

the words, 'You only think you know me.'
Some leaves will not peel back, the basement

fills with loam and serpents
you can't interpret.

Each baby's head will feast inside
a purse of a bed, wet breast and head.

In this chaos of emotion, all fresh
in cotton

will grow the G-d of old. But you cannot
look a face in the face and live

to be understood, I'm told.

Flamingo pink on the chimney stacks
On bushes too beaten with snow
It's Saturn's morning, accumulation
During the single hours, enormous

Mixed clouds are more propitious than fleece
And the poor who are occluded
and stationary will tell the true story

If, white Papa, you'll turn
Your dark face towards us

The Milennium ends, you nonetheless weep
Oh God this life was full of failure
To say thanks
That unconscious body you're holding is mine
Open my heart for the night, it's empty

Three hundred and twenty eight more days
Are due this year and even with that many lives

I'd still have only one history

I didn't read enough to recognize my own cliches.
Was instead an active ricochet —

passionate lines at the oaken
table, sent off, later to return, folded.

In this next-to-lowest state, a wall
approximates the wills inside: one's daily dread
was poverty (another child)

the other's was, I wasn't adored
except if I tried it, by the Lord

whose shadow vaulted the tables and things,
or hid, under them, with the kids.

It's cloudy down south thickening
Like windows up high
What should I tell the teens and those smaller

Your jump suit is inadequate for a fall
Low-life manners will buck you sideways
Work on details and aim for higher elevations

If spirited away by urban guerillas
You might finally settle with the past
By drawing from the future

A lid of snow, like a thin sawblade
A jeweler uses to cut a ring
Blows diamonds around

So starting a new day alone
Feels like a rough sketch
Of yourself being distributed to the media

Clear, cloudy, clear, cloudy, clear, rain, clear

Walls make a space the opposite
of lost, but this is false.

Up Robeson Street a blight was on
the oaks in Franklin Park where Olmsted planned

to hold some land apart for paradise.
But in the zoo an animal
killed his keeper same time I wanted to kill mine,

and this stage was really hell — the fracas of an el
to downtown Boston, back out again,

with white boys banging the lids of garbage cans,
calling racial zingers into our artificial lights

and leaves which naturally dizzied and fell.

14

Love essays, in the form of Eros
To be at liberty and in the dark
An armful of kisses

While every third hope is shot
Down with the cold of a faraway Moscow

Anyway emotion rises between
As lobsters roll up from the ocean

Do steer clear of an indifferent climate
You have so many duties to attend to
Extreme factors help a lot

Ponder God's love and not your memory
Soon — if you're a good thinker —
You will identify the trap in your feelings

Even before they are tested
You who've been for freedom this long long time

You check the river, I check the garden
See one mile in snow and fog

On the rendering you go over tomorrow
The engineer's blueprint of the bowshape
Now the moon is nearing her full phase

It's partly navy, windy and cold
You in the privacy of your study reproduce
Another polka-dotted package

So the ideal wins the heart
As a friend who has power

Gets lost. Inside your mind, history
Has opened a hand full of light

Asking, Will you join me for a toast?
Well, I feel I'm falling through the sky

It's three o'clock in the a.m.
When thinkers play low, a major sin
In bridge, as in bridge-building

Sometimes I think you'll never grow up
For my sake
The upper half of your system is a ridge
Of high pressure. Prepare against

Attack by fate or romance, and who else is
Cognizant of your failures but your cousinly me?

Chastity makes them children together
Comfortless. Squint and variable cloudiness
Will reveal an idea whose time is here

Costly errors. Financial concerns
We also have inner conflict

It's just the hour when you want
A friend to sit on a deck and recollect
With, while the sun goes down

Meantime seas are building to six feet offshore
And you are thinking of taking a trip

Let someone else handle the problems
Is how you're living now, it's insane

It wasn't dawn until the cock had crowed.
This way an ear or mind

can undermine the spirit, and make matter
worse.

If the prospect of the Gospel eye'd allow it,
nature would go on this way I guess

pretty much the same.

But what wilt thou, soul, do
to excite my soul again in me?

Please like sweet flowers —
the pansy and the perfect daisy —
let the inside feel to be.

Not windblown around the furnishings.
These things, and all efforts of failure,

they haunt me.

My work was my delight alongside
the children. I left home's hard

protective touch, for this necessity.
If I'm a failure

at poetry and perfection
goes to another (the one beside me exactly)

what will I say to
one whole unbelievable past?

Desire constructs a shuddering side, no rest.
You want the soul's approval, most, but sigh

to have, as well, good looks,
character, love, money, success and just desserts

which mainly depend on luck, not work.

No time spent on fiction,
or psychology, but poetry and Simone Weil

let me know how well
landscape and architecture

adhere to the terms of desire and nothing else.
Does. That must be why I left

the place and then came back
to rake it up. The halls showed a grave

and thick collapse of boughs, emotion too!
and none of the mulch would move.

My soul climbed overhead, then up and out
to the blue, while time stood by, below,

unable to follow.

Never stop at a motel where some of the vacancy
Lights are out if you feel terrible
And have no sympathy
Cards coming. Play the radio, discard all drinks
Temporize by holding your own suit
Such as it is
Bitter belief! That nature is revolting
And empty of emotional or metaphoric content

If the Quebec peninsula is only making waves
What is friendship
Snake-eyes, the deuce of spades

Refugees from the steamy climate come to
Massachusetts concerned about humidity, how
Your blessing is their bad weather
Chance of swans, they read the sky

God's snow is spread across the coast
It visits someone in pain and bed, plays host

Grief you named that time
When the evening stars are Venus and Mars
And pockets of blue snow assemble

But the association isn't sure
What happened to the real world and your idea
is herewith returned as undeliverable

The planets will tell you to seek out friends
Between Worcester and Hyannis today

But I say, Be a servant always
And never a slave, and you'll know what grief is
You'll have the word

THE NURSERY

The baby
         was made in a cell
in the silver & rose underworld.
Invisibly prisoned
                  in vessels & cords, no gold
for a baby; instead
eyes, and a sudden soul, twelve weeks
old, which widened its will.

Tucked in the notch of my fossil: bones
        laddered a spine from a cave,
the knees & skull
were etched in this cell, no stone, no gold
where no sun brushed its air.

One in one, we slept together
        all sculpture
                of two figures welded.
But the infant's fingers
squeezed & kneaded
                me, as if to show
the Lord won't crush what moves
on its own . . . secretly.

On Robeson Street
                    anonymous
was best, where babies
have small hearts
                    to learn
with;
          like intimate
thoughts on sea
water, they're limited.

Soldered to my self
    it might be a soldier or a thief
for all I know.
The line between revolution & crime
    is all in the mind
        where ideas of righteousness
and rights confuse.

I walked the nursery floor.
By four-eyed buttons & the curdle of a cradle's
paint: a trellis of old gold
    roses, lipped & caked
where feet will be kicking in wool.

        Then the running,
the race after,
cleaning the streets, up for a life.
His technicolor cord
hung from a gallery of bones,
    but breathing, *I'm finished.*
    Both of us.

And when the baby sighed,
through his circle of lips,
                    I kissed it,
        and so did he, my circle to his,
we kissed ourselves and each other,
        as if each cell was a Cupid,
        and we were born in it.

The cornerstone's dust
up-floating

by trucks & tanks.
White flowers spackle

the sky crossing the sea.
A plane above the patio

wakes the silence
and my infant who raises

his arms to see
what he's made of.

O animation! O liberty!

FRANKLIN PARK

When snow falls on Franklin Park
and black grackles —

North, South, Central — sit between
each invisible spot of
happiness — the mothers walk by, brutally

into the old autumn gush of rust
red leaves

like you should be lucky to grow old
at all. I still see them, more of us.

Puddingstone, rutty and tough, in snow under their feet
turns into a soft thing thrown down

over the edge of dried myrtle and beech
leaves. Cars whir and curse

in front of what used to be our house
before our fortunes were reversed.

This America is a wonderful place,
one immigrant said. If it's a cage, then it's safe.

Down Robeson Street, away
from the park and zoo,

     bends become
   calamities of bricked-up
   capital: those who
doze, mid-afternoon, meditate

bright close to time's receding

     glance and out.
     There's drink on the shelf,
grain in the pantry so the Padre

says it's not poverty we're getting used to

Refrigerators hum like animals
     running to music. A cutting
     wind rattles
out numbers, and minds organize
   each margin's going . . .

but it's just, he said, we got used to being.

Sprung out of sticks, fourteen lilacs
   hung over my fence from the tenement
next door.
            Once, when pregnant,
   and all for freedom,
       I shook the rain off the wet, blue
flowers
          and knew why it was that I was pregnant:
          more lips to love more lilacs with.

Permanent — for life —
where technical

requirements —
science, influence,

physical strength
and dignity

apply day to day —
is the small

variable according
to age and society

race and economy —
bent on a bench

a cliche — like "crumbs"
of anonymity

marked only
by proximity

to birds, beasts
and St. Francis.

In Franklin Park a daughter
held onto the swing

while a ward of the State,
a boy in frayed pants and shirt

for wiping dirt, his hair
snipped short, as if it were war,

watched me push, her pump.
Thin and whiter than most children,

he was motherless. Suddenly
she jumped into the red

leaves falling, her wild will
access to emergency.

My rage — always on call —
she never guessed was love,

she tells me now,
though I saw *he* knew.

As a guard in a baggy suit
is to a prisoner of politics,

so is wandering this park
to the eyes of a face like his,

wretched with exile's knowledge

and given — Pretorian —
to large shoes, a spare shirt.

Gone is the brush of dustball
curls, miniature clothes,

and vanished is the Cape of Good Hope.
Is somebody's son, yet.

Home to him's now a sandpaper map
of his mother's playground
credo: *expect nothing*

and put everything in its place.
Freedom's behind your face.

The free child's swinging
as from interior pumpkins:
   all strings attached
      invisible, and the orange of
each smoky thing is good, enough.

Prison's not in the mind
of small hands on cold chains
   . . . but brick
red and yellow, builds and falls
     with the child trying

and the clouds flying.

Pushing children in plaid & silver prams
us mothers were dumpy,
                    hunched in the damp

and our redlipped infants
    sucked on their strange fingers
        eyes stunned by the gunny-strong
            grass on near hills.

I wanted to sit near sweet water, or salt
in the fuzz of extreme weather,
        but we're not here to.

Like women who love the Lord live on hills

what for, what for, we cawed outside
        as in bare trees, too plain to see.

In the sylvan section of the old zoo,
        some of us pace and traffic,
                pushing carriages
up the avenue

while others do
        baseball and barbecue, near where
        the primate cage is closed.

Birds pulsate in a repulsive
replica of the tropics, as if painted, can't breathe.

It's the end of afternoon, when all things blacken.

        I say, Fix me a rum and coke
and a good strong smoke, Mr. No One.
                Me and the kids are looking to go home now.

The snowflakes whirled, miniscule,
and three storey tenements
seemed to eat what was due

to the children in windows: pink lips
open on glass and frost . . . No sky
upstairs, but a wall surrounding

walls and a woman . . . Like this

happiness learned to be lonely before it could be lost and
No, no opiate made so many people as poor as this but pure
desire. And to those few I must say *yes* to their wish,
"Let my experience make me famous or rich." Your emptiness
  will come too, follow you from home and everywhere

the courage to suffer is missing.

PALMS

First a green opening,
mottled apples
viewed from above.

Was time of recovery.
Rain, that's life, on a bed
of red Mission flowers.

But when the danger passed,
dozens, but dozens, of more
insignia grew, the appetite

for comfort, went looking,
inner, tonal,

for where the green begins,
to where there's nothing,
but nothing.

The wounds were balmed
around a palm and lizards

froze on one of two
two-by-fours.
Walls, but access
where salt off excess

pain was held, like a head
holds in what it can't get out.

Some algebraic thinking
spiked the shock of suffering.

It's when too much has happened,
more must be done.

Reason for the palm
leaves moved too fast to see;
and the question's out a candle.

Wind leaned its atoms on my cheek;
it's all Greek to me:

how motion is
like comfort's
only goal — to prove, where I was,
I'm not now, is all I know.

Same as love & work,
much time's spent,
splitting a vacuum.

Zeno saw, in his law,
an immortal immobility.

Birds succumbed to the regimen
of dots & found they were nowhere.

Worries & also words
bump through such dots, and blow

stark emblems on dangerous naughts.
Once stopped, they seem to be

gone, like an angel's position
is motionless. Can't see it once,

or only always.

I have to say it: character's no rock,
not after all's uncovered, wild

& tragic in its disappearing logic.

So much calumny is auto-
mechanic, its victim wearies
of the traffic, changes course too.

You enter history

as words come into the air,
first letters first, and so on,
backwards.

Caught in a war of yes against no
stands pity. It never moves
is why you can't see it.

There's some hum
as up from a grassy serpent,
makes pity look & look.

Dread's at work,
against, not for it.

Dread's out hunting pulses;
but pity's the one
that doesn't bat an eyelash:

more static than static.

About lonely angels
after a war: they carry candles

and the night street clicks
with wings, jokes & little heels. On a

banner: INRI, in regard to, Ah,
you know who. Still coming

till then. Of poverty's course,
if you keep working, it feels worse.

Sore shoes on soft feet, as if
more's always too much, but less.

Stamp the Logos on the air,
father, next time, now.

Simple faith's a way not given
statement. Wonder sinks to golden
silence. Children

are abundant, ripen,
and some fall.

This way
order's order's all hidden,
or left to formulation:

pyramid & graph
scrawled on a diagram's dare.

MISSION HILL

Gray victory
garden, a chicken
wire fence: early Mass

The yellow projects
dawn near tumbledown
weeds

A Rican rooster cocks
at a crow, an American
car idles

outside the basilica

Big plantation, big city

Borders of bells:
deliver us from evil

A splinter of luck
pricks at
the suffering of others

Unsensual usuals
govern faces in traumatic
action. The Jesus is out

where scaffolding knocks & church

goers at the poor box, drop
the hope of timber in

the void. It's a paradox
box, contains
both food & absolutes

Censor race
difference; it's poverty
homestyle, where

we're drinking out in
the rain

Water so pure, so clear
Soaked in the mud, ashes
of one who said:

"Work on what you know
for the unknown is near"

Gullies of labor,

wash down the tracks
between fair & unfair

Garcia's popcorn
yellow store, in a rainy night:

Colors & things
the people move among, damp,
sensuous, counting money

A small brown girl with missing teeth
I like to think of

her happiness, safe
atmosphere of commerce, her mother's

work accomplished
and observed, the power of bliss

The fast lane of a life
goes so slow you never see

how trees burn up seasons
in fatal order, like Olmsted's
chain of parks

meant to last forever:
now stripped, discolored

Still, no human fate
on his plan might mean

realism has oppressed again . . .
Oh God, don't abandon those whom you have made

Proximity of prayer
is like a little well's
way into the beautiful

black. Here, words drill
a path for a sailing soul — if —

the sky has ears

Writing with stars
the spirit dabbles
where endings never are

But somewhere a donkey's warm
chewing on grass

It's where,
sweet earth, the soul aspires, back

Hispanic neon
gilds the image of

gold when lonely
dreads — night & day —
put Mary and candles

in one place.

Up for anyone's grab,
all day
in dusk the heart slows down

and the real world yearns to pause.
Even a store,
after a day's labor —

objects in rows & boxes
and the salesman's perfume —

puts the "heaven" back into having.

At Robeson Street,
at home, the children
emptied their chests

for toys in song.
Howled
in double-prams

and slept
with pulsing chests.

In cold light
on the brittle

leaves, they laughed
and let me know: No.

Little on earth compares with breath.

JOY HAD I KNOWN BEFORE

For not having died yet
Knowing my cherished wish
Will not make the necessary changes
To accommodate me to it
Or you, I'm glad
Rooms replete with mystery and routine
Yens remind me of approaching
Old age in dereliction
Of children I could have had and known
If I had married before
The one whose name is Addiction

Outside snow decays the country
Browns of fertile mud's lowliness
Or the storms of Labrador
Blow the doors of heaven closed
The sunshine index drops to zero
And electric light is solo
Cheer along with other scientific things
The wind brings
Scattered flurries
Freezing spray and I'm living
When I hear your voice say *Joy*
Had I known before.

POETRY FROM ALICE JAMES BOOKS